83-177

Y		C142
2		
Zd	Zdenck, Marilee	

AUTHOR	God is a Verb
TITLE	

DATE DUE	BORROWER'S NAME	ROOM NUMBER

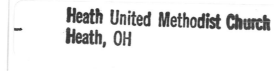

Heath United Methodist Church
Heath, OH

89

God is a Verb!

God is a Verb!

words by marilee zdenek
action by marge champion

Word Books, Publisher

Waco, Texas

Library of Congress catalog card number: 74-82663

In the beginning was the Verb,
  and the Verb was with God,
and the Verb was God.*

—*John 1:1*

*translated literally from the Spanish:
En el principeo era el Verbo, y el Verbo era con Dios, y el Verbo era Dios.

This book is dedicated to you, Lord—

Why not?

After all, each poem was prayer-tested before it was written.

Over the years
          we have delighted in you
               argued with you
               followed you and
               occasionally ignored you—

But oh, my Lord,
          how much we have loved you!

You've led me to some hairy places, Lord—
            when I've followed you
            in that free-fall ecstasy of faith.

When I find myself hung up somewhere,
            entangled in the cords I didn't see,
I wonder if you led me there at all—
            or if I have a talent
            for landing in swamps and trees.

I'm willing, Jesus,
            to follow where you lead,
But we need to get our signals straight—
There's just no point
                        in jumping out there by myself
                        thinking you're in front of me
                        then getting there and finding
                        it was someone else.

I'm dangling by a slender thread of hope,
            with faith the size of a rivet bolt some days.

I believe in your promises, Lord,
I'm not blaming you when I misread the lines . . .
            but I'd like a course in navigation,
            a few more lessons in interpreting the signs.

In the meantime,
I'd like to let you know,
In spite of all the times I've screwed things up—
I really do appreciate
                        the steady holding power of your love.

I'd like to make peace with all the dragons in my head—
all those dark creatures
who came in the open door of childhood
and bedded down.

I've denied them, feared them, and fought them.
All the same, I've fed them rather well.

They've grown fat on my hatred,
Multiplied like rabbits in the warm nest of my obsession,
Overpopulated my psyche with their kids.

I'm very kind to other people's dragons,
   it's my own I'm not able to forgive.

I'm holding all my dragons by their tails—
   I'd like to meet them face to face,
    get to know them,
      where they came from,
        why they came.

It's hard to love my enemies, Lord—
To make peace with intrusive creatures
   who moved in first
   then signed those long-term leases In my head.

Please come in and help me face the dragons.
   (Help me not to run if they breathe a little fire.)
I'd like to meet a really scaly monster,
     shake his hand
     maybe even smile.

You know I'm not some princess in a palace, who thinks it's rather nice
   to kiss a frog.
But if I learn to love that ugly dragon,
   could you change him to a prince before too long?

It was a glorious dawn—
and for a change I got a running leap on the morning
and saw the sun paint halleluiah in the sky.

I want to open my arms and embrace the promises and claim the joys.

I want to do some things my inhibitions won't allow—

like jumping Ms. McGurdy's five foot wall
and shouting SURPRISE to see if that will make her smile.

Like dancing up the supermarket aisles

leaping over shopping carts

vaulting right over reality to see

that joy is not so fleeting after all.

I'm very good at celebrating, Lord—
Have you noticed?
My soul can fly so high above the world
        I could play in a field of clouds
        and nestle like a child in the comfort of your love.

I can laugh with delight at your miracles—
Sing to the sunset
Dance 'til the sunrise
Whistle in the sunshine of your care.

But in other times
When the pendulum swings
And darkness is upon the face of my day,

Then, Lord—
Please come
And teach me how to celebrate.

My friend died.

I don't understand you, God.
I don't understand your timetables
        where the living dead live on and long to die
        and one so young, so filled with life and love is gone.

I have to deal with sorrow in my own way.
From the crest of a skier's hill, I need to race the pain
        outrun the tears
        rush past the anger and the loss—

        but the speed of grief transcends my need
        and leaves me spent and lonely still.

Now on this frozen, silent hill,
        I lay my grief before you to be healed.

Lord, I can find no answers, help me to find acceptance.
Though the pain remains,
        let the new day begin for me without bitterness.

You are the healing
the loving
the touching

You are the laughing
You are the dancing

Jesus, Verb of God
You are the moving—
move in me.

All week the sounds of the city bombarded my ears—
        traffic sounds
        people sounds
        expansion sounds
        endless sounds.

I escaped on Friday to the beach and slept on soft sand
        listening to the twigs crackling in the fire beside me,
        warming me and humming in the darkness.

Then—come morning—
        listening to the gulls
        and the breakers calling
        for some lone surfer to come and play,

            I took my board and drifted far beyond the breakers swells

                and listened

                and drank in the silence

                becoming one with the stillness

                until—

Finally, I sought the wave to take me home,
Heard the rumbling ocean thunder of the breaker's warning call,
Caught the crest and rode it to the shore.

Thank you for the day, Lord, for the night—
        for being here beside me in the quiet.

Come with me now, back to the city again,
And teach me to hear your voice
        within the traffic sounds
        people sounds
        expansion sounds
        endless sounds
        of life.

I've stretched so far, Lord,
       extending myself to the limit.
       Now I'm hurting and need a time to pull back
       and consider what I'm striving for.

Well, I put my whole self in—
       to causes
       programs
       and projects.

Now I'll take my whole self out—for a while,
       to evaluate priorities,
       to get in touch with my feelings and my needs.

Work with me, Jesus,
       and let me see what you and I
       are going to do with me.

I want to be known as I am,
        not loved for the best of myself
        but in spite of the worst.

Somedays I want to cry out:
        Look, I'm hurting behind this confident guise.
        Listen, not to my words that say I'm doing fine
        but to the silences that are sighs without sound.
        Feel with me, not just when success is mine
        but when I'm threatened or I've failed.

In this game-playing world
        I want to be real.
        Why do I still hide behind the smile
        that protects me and isolates me
        at the same time?

You were so vulnerable, Jesus—
        standing before the world without a mask,
        letting them see that when you felt anger you showed it,
                when you felt sorrow you wept.

Didn't you know you had an image to protect?
Didn't you worry that they would mistake
        humanness for weakness
        weakness for failure
        failure for lack of worth?

Your openness astounds me . . .
        and challenges me.

I believe in you, Jesus,
        help me to believe in myself.

I wonder what's at the top of the rope?
It's hard to climb with no foothold
                and no end in sight,
                to work so hard for every inch I gain.

What will I find when I get there?
Will it be worth the price—
                the ache of shoulders that must hold my weight
                                with endless strain
                the activity of hands that can't let go
                                long enough to pick a flower
                the concentration of my mind
                                that dare not wander lest I slip and fall?

Is it worth all that
                and more—
                the loneliness that comes
                because there isn't room for anyone
                beside me as I climb?

What's at the top of the rope, Lord?

God, I feel pushy!

I always want things MY WAY—
Why am I so sure I know what's best?

I can't stand what I see—
              ME—running around playing God in someone else's life.

Even if I'm right,
What right do I have to manipulate,
              to maneuver someone else's plans?

Lord, help me to keep my hands off things that don't belong to me—
Like other people's lives.

It's a beautiful world for exploring, Lord.
Joys are hidden like tiny jewels
                within the moments of the day,
                            there to touch
                            to keep
                            or just to hold a while and then replace.

I've taken a winding course
                to treasure hunt through deepest caves
                to search for some exotic shell
                            golden coin
                            or rare exquisite pearl.

When I think of all the places where I've been
                            the things I've done
                            the people that I've loved
                            the serendipities that came
                                            from time to time—
I know the search itself
                has more value
                            than the find.

"I can pray," said my child,
"Anywhere I am,
Even riding on my bike without my hands!"

Little girl, if you believe that
                then you have learned a lesson well,

And God will ride with you
                and walk with you
                and dance with you
                and smile.

There you go—
                spinning cartwheels—
                                touching the cool earth with your hands,
                                feeling the new grass sprout between your fingers,
                                reaching to the heavens with your toes.

There you go—
                with a giggle and a prayer,
                walking with Jesus on a day that isn't Sunday,
                                in a place that isn't special,
                                in your grubby jeans
                                and tangled wind-tossed hair.

Lord, I'm so glad she doesn't need some formal kind of prayer,
For Tammy's learned to talk with you
                                while standing on her head,
And Tammy's learned to feel you near
                                while doing cartwheels in the air.

cond Presbyterian Church
Church and Second Sts.
Newark , Ohio 43055

I've finally made peace with the struggle—

Who wants a life with all the questions answered,
                   all the dilemmas solved?

Who wants to wake up in the morning and find
        there is no great issue to wrestle with that day?

I would go out of my skull, Lord,
                       with a simple life.

I'm not made for it—
How could I part with all my problems?
      We have become inseparable over the years.

Who needs all that peace and tranquility?

Me.

I've been told that some things are sacred
and some things are secular—
but those are confusing terms.

So I looked up the word "secular"
and the dictionary said:
"things connected with the world;
things not religious or sacred."

Isn't that a contradiction of terms?
What is more sacred than life?
Isn't work sacred, Jesus? And laughter—
Isn't all that touches your brothers touching you?

You must have been doing your father's will
when you worked as a carpenter in Joseph's shop.

You were about your father's business
talking with rabbis in the temple
dining with whores and tax collectors
playing with children
sailing with fishermen
forgiving sins and healing lepers.

Tell me, Jesus—
which part of your life was sacred;
which part was concerned with the world?

And in my life—
speak to me of today
and tell me,
what part of it
does not concern you?

Where am I going, Lord?
Racing through life at full speed,
Fearing the mundane more than the unknown.
Where am I headed in such a hurry?
            Is it your work I rush so fast to do—
            or is it dull routine I race so frantically to avoid?

I feel the challenge
            the excitement
            the adrenalin flow
            and at that moment never doubt the call.

But in still hours, when the night finds me weary and spent,
            I wonder—
            where did all that racing around get me?
            What was all the hurrying for?

I need to feel your hand on the throttle of my life,
I need another look at your road map, Lord.

Some people seem to think I have a problem.

They say I'm stubborn—
        that I don't know when to quit.
        How do they figure it?
                If we're not tenacious,
                        where do we get?

Maybe I am a little willful,
                but obstinate is much too strong a word.
Just because I tend to see things through,
                I don't think I'm stubborn Lord,
                    do you?

Everything's piling up on me, Lord.
It's the week before Christmas
            and I did it again—
            waited too late
            and the stores are jammed
            with people just like me
            . . . wishing it was over.

I know a woman who shops for Christmas in July
            and addresses her cards in August.

That really turns me off, Jesus—
            eleven months of the year.
            But in the twelfth month I wonder—

                        what's it all about?
                        All the weary shoppers
                        all the frantic clerks
                        all the bunions bulging from their sockets.

What ever happened to peace on earth?

Where will she find her dream, Lord?

Where will she be when you whisper in her ear and say,
  "Hey, Gina, look over here?"

Will you speak to her in quiet times when she's alone—
  Or in the burst of a breaker's foam
  on an August day
  when the beach is filled with kids
      who seek and dream and doubt
      and listen for some voice to speak to them of hope?

We would hold her gently with our love
  and try to be a shelter
      in these stormy times
      where she can feel the safety of our home.
We would hold her loosely in our hands
  that her soul will be kept free
  to sail to distant lands
  to explore
  to learn
  to dream—
  free to leave, and to return.

We would like to do that, Lord
But it's very hard—
And underneath those grown-up woman ways
  there's still a little girl
  whose boat's so small and when the sky is dark
      sometimes, I am afraid.
Watch over her as she goes
      racing through the turbulence
      of teen-age seas—
And help us trust you, Jesus, with her voyage.

45

I like an open door for children in our home,
       where they can come and go with friends
       and know there's always room
       for more faces at the table—
       more sleeping bags on the floor.

I like a house that's full of kids
                and giggles
                and music
                and joy.

But on days when it's not like that at all
       and the house is full of tattling
                tempers
                and tears,
                then, Lord—

hang in there with me,
give me the wisdom of Solomon
the patience of Job
the perception of Freud
or Lord . . .
   if you think I'm asking too much,
   then just give me the faith
         to relax in you
         and the insight to remember how it was.

It's mine!
I got the job—
It came like a bolt
When I didn't expect it.
Now that I have it
I'm scared.
Everyone wants it
How can I hold it?

If I play it cool, I'll be fine.
Don't let me psyche myself out, Lord—

It's mine!

49

Lord, I'm up to my eyeballs with PEOPLE.
I want to scream—
shout STOP IT to the whole wide world.
I feel out of control
unforgiving
misunderstood
exasperated with everyone for pulling me in seventy directions at once.

I can't stretch that far, Lord,
I can't meet everybody's needs,
                be all things to all people
                be available all the time.

I can't slam doors
                bellow
                swear even, without the pangs of guilt.
Something's struggling inside me to be born and I feel torn—
                caught between motherhood and selfhood
                idealism and reality
                high goals and low thresholds.

Very quietly, Lord,
I would like to go off in the garage
                take an old set of cracked dishes
                and smash them against the wall.

I won't—
But, oh my Lord, how I would love to!

She's eighty-five years old, Lord—
        eighty-five and going strong on the hottest day in July!

        I sit around doing nothing
        but grumbling about the heat.

        It makes me think—

If I quit complaining long enough to consider how I felt,
        I might react differently to how I feel.

Waiting for the temperature to change
        is part of a larger problem—

        of waiting for tomorrow
                to feel the joy
        waiting until I have time
                to discover my full potential
        waiting until it's convenient with everyone else
                to explore the depths of talent in myself.

        Waiting
                waiting
                        waiting

        for something else to change.

I'm trembling, Lord,
        the world is shaky for me now.
Everywhere I turn I feel the doubt—
        Which way is safe?
        Which way holds me firm?
        What small move could send me over the precipice
                into the emptiness
                with no way of return?

Hold me, Lord,
Steady me with your promises,
        that I may touch them
        and believe them
        once more.

You touched me—
        and the world didn't change—
        but I began to.

You touched me—
        and the valley didn't go away—
        but I looked up and saw a mountain range.

You touched me—
        and since you did, I haven't been the same.

I'm going all the way with you, Lord,
I'm not holding back anymore.
I'm soaring to the summit of your plan
        leaping into life
        flying on the high jumps to your hand.

I have this mushy thing about anniversaries.
I get this funny feeling every time.

> So here I sit, Lord—
> just like last year,
> trying to write
> a few profound lines.
> It shouldn't be so hard
> to write a card
> to tell my guy I love him
> that I'm glad we got it together
> and kept it going all these years.

Page after page is crumpled in a heap.
All my tender feelings
Come out sounding maudlin,
All my adoration
Comes out gooey sweet.

I can't funnel all my caring
Into a dinky card;
Give me inspiration, Lord—

I don't want to say it with Hallmark.

It was one of those days when all the waters in the heavens
        poured down on Texas
        like some celestial water main burst in the sky.

I remember, Lord,
How I sat in school that day
        and listened to the sound of rain bombarding the roof
                burbling through the drain pipe
                pummeling the mud puddles below.
Some kids were playing hooky,
        running through the gushing gutters,
        I kept thinking I could almost hear them laugh.

Lightning charged through fierce black clouds,
Thunder roared like the king of the sky.
It made me wonder about your creations
        and the mysteries you flaunted in that storm.
        What made the lightning fly?
        Where was the rain before it fell?

It made me wonder about myself,
Wonder who I was and would be.
Could I write a poem or a book?
Would my own work have value?
Would I have value without my work?

        And then the teacher said:
        "Are you daydreaming again!
        How many times must you be told?
        Pay attention to what I'm saying.
        Sit up straight and face the front.
        You haven't heard one word I've said.
        Won't you be sorry when you can't answer
        the questions on my test!"

It was a long time, Lord,
Before I wondered my rainy day questions again.

Please make spaces in my soul, Jesus—
Huge spaces,
                    to make room for new ideas, surprises, and dreams.
Spaces for quiet—
                    without one sound at all.
Silence has been squeezed out of our times
                    by man-made noise
                                        and needs space to be.

There are those who feel
                    that spaces must be quickly filled with something.
                    And they are disturbed
                                        by spaces in talking when nothing's said,
                                        spaces on walls with nothing on them,
                                        spaces in life
                                                            that hold one still
                                                            —becalmed for a while
                                                            until the wind begins again
                                                            until the sails are filled.

There are those who do not understand spaces—
                    who say that children do not grieve for long.
                    Those who say that
                                        do not know children
                                        and are deceived
                                                            by children putting laughter
                                                            in the spaces between their tears.

I loved my uncle's ranch when I was a child.
        There was space to run unhampered
        and freedom to explore.

The dust lay inches thick upon the trails
        and running barefoot down a path of sifted powder
        was a sumptuous sort of feel.

The barn was my playground full of animated toys,
The loft was full of hay and mice and fairly friendly spiders.

The mint grew wild and plush beside the creek.
My aunt made berry pies
        and the smell would seek me out
            anywhere I played around the house.

I rode my cousin's palomino horse
        through fantasies that never seemed to end.

If I'm careful, Lord, I can edit these thoughts and forget
        that I got a bee sting when I picked the mint
        and burned my tongue time and again on the berry pies
            because I never seemed to learn and couldn't wait
        that the barn smelled just awful
        and the horse made my bottom sore
        and the dust that felt like sifted powder
            made me sneeze all summer.

If I'm careful, I can forget these things.

But if I'm wise,
        I can remember that all of life has both things in it
        and I may choose which part to hold to me.

It's hard to juggle with valuables, Lord—
        to keep so many plates in the air,
        husband,
            children,
                work,
                    friends—
Somewhere there should be a plate named for
ME.

There's such delicate timing involved,
Help me to keep them in balance, Lord.

In careless hands
People I love
        could shatter, too.

Second Presbyterian Church
Church and Second Sts.
Newark, Ohio 43055

What can I claim as mine, Lord?
            Not people
            nor money
            nor things
                        for all of these can die or turn to ashes in the night.

    So what is mine—
                except my feelings
                my memories
                and you?

He's bringing guests for dinner!
Oh, God . . . how could he?
It's already after five,
> and I've been running around all day.
> The house looks like the moving van just left
> and there's one head of lettuce and the roast
>> left from last night.

Lord . . . how COULD he!

Will we have enough if I cut it in chunks
> with onion and garlic and wine . . .
> and a can of mushrooms to stretch it some?

Lord—did I ever thank you for cans?
> of mandarin oranges
> and lichee nuts
> cans of French beans
> and cans of biscuits
> cans of cherries for jubilee—

> dear God, how thankful I am for these.

And when I'm finished being angry
> I'll be thankful again for him.

How can he help it if he opens his heart and the world pours in?
He opens our lives to quick celebrations
> drop-in friends and spontaneous plans
> where strangers enter now and then
>> share our table
>> and leave as friends.

Three times, I'm sure,
When our home was shared with strangers
> we entertained an angel, unawares.

For:
   a creative spring that burst through the barren winter,
   implosions of hope and explosions of joy,
   a new chance each morning,
   and sometimes—
   heaven now.
            Thanks, Lord

There's so much going on in Blake's head—
     I see him thinking
     and I wonder
     but he never says.
     He's a quiet one
     with twinkling eyes
     and a touch of mischief but he smiles
          at cats.
          And people—if you look before he ducks his head.

His days are filled with trampolines and drums,
     karate chops and basketballs and bikes.

Blake has secrets running around in that head.
     Does he share them with you, Lord?
     Does he know you're a neat guy who understands
     about little boys becoming men?

He's a neat guy too, Lord—
My friend Blake.

I'm drowning, Jesus, in a sea of loneliness.

People in shallow waters watch—
               as in a dream, I scream—
                             the faces smile.

Strong waves of longing beat against the shore,
               catching me in the undertow
               sucking me into the vastness of the ocean's force.

If I can relax and go with the tide
               drift with the current
               will I survive?

       Will you be there if I float free?
       Will you be there to help me reach the shore?

I can't reach him Lord.

The awareness of it came like an icy wind that startled the summer.
I hear the irritation when we talk
            of little things
            that in themselves
            could never bring such coldness to his voice.

How long has it been since I saw his sudden smile
                              for no reason
                              except that our eyes met?

How long has it been since he found a way to touch me
            while passing coffee
            morning papers
            and time?

I want to stretch out my hand and touch the security of his love.
I want to reach across the distance of our busy lives
            and feel him reach for me
            and need me as I need him.

Bless us, Lord, with the healing power of your love.

What happened to all the easy answers?
   Things used to be so black and white—
   things were wrong or they were right,
      then life came along and showed me gray.

I'm having trouble with gray, Lord—
   My placid stream of absolutes became a raging river
      as more and more of black and white
         became absorbed in gray.

I'm living in the rapids, Lord,
   with changing forces all around.
   I can't go back to where I was
      when simple answers were enough
      when each cliché made sense to me
      and "right is right" was just a fact of life.

Now in this day of complexity,
   ambivalence and diversity,
   my only total certainty
   is
   You.

I heard the piping but did not dance;
I heard the wailing but did not mourn.
Wrapped up tightly in my own world, I heard with my ears—
                                        but not with my heart.

Forgive me, Lord.

In your whole symphony of life,
        I want to go with the high notes and the low,
        responding to each sound in the total song,
        playing your music,
        letting the sound of your love
        be the refrain
        that repeats itself
        in my life—
        extending to all the lives
        that my life touches.

The sun chased the darkness from the sky.
This day has come to claim its fractional share of eternity—
and so have I.

I want to say yes to new beginnings
yes to the Comforter
yes to the healing
yes to the table of bread and of wine
yes to songs and laughter
yes to the Son of man
yes to the challenges—YES TO LIFE!

I know a man so free—
            so sure of his own worth
            that he accepts it
            with neither pride nor humility.

He's so sure of who he is
            and the value of his work
            that his wife is free to explore the horizons of her life.

He's not afraid she may reach some mountaintop without him,
            or love him less as her interests grow.

                    He puts up with dinners that are sometimes late.
                    The house isn't as tidy as it was before—
                            but she laughs more
                            and has more to say at the end of the day
                            when he comes home to a woman
                                        who has opened a door
                                        unseen before—
                            who wants him to look with her
                                        and wonder. . . .

                    I know a man so free—
                    And best of all,
                    He loves me.

The wind of the Spirit is blowing,
    lift me, Lord, and let me soar with the speed of tim
    content to see the dust of yesterday bury the past.

Chase the wind with me,
Dream with me,
Yesterday is gone and can't be held by wishes.
Now is the time for vision and for prayer,
This is a day for new adventures
                I do rejoice,
                        and I am glad.

It's a brand new day, Jesus,
        a shining Sunday that's just been born
        and has only twenty-four hours to live it up.
This day is a special one for me
        for no reason except that I choose to make it special
                and the choice is mine.
Today I want to tune into my feelings and accept them,
        to wake the joy that lies sleeping beneath a blanket of everydayness
        and say, "It's time to get up and celebrate—
        this is the Lord's day—and mine!"
I want to worship you, Lord, with all the stops out,
        to sing a hymn like I mean it for a change,
        to dance with tambourines and drums and shouts of joy,
                just like you told us to in olden days.
I want to dance like David and pray like Paul
        and find out what halleluliah really means.
Help me to shake loose from my hang-ups
        and feel the freedom to be spontaneous and fully alive.
Today I want to go to church, unafraid to laugh or cry
        or show the human feelings that I hold inside.
And when the hour has ended, please make the meaning of it last
Help me to be free to touch a stranger with my eyes without shyness,
                free to touch a lonely person with my hands in your name,
                free to do whatever I feel like doing that honors you.
I'd like to paint a prayer on a kite and fly it over Houston.
I wish I flew a plane so I could use the vapor trail to write,
        "I love you, Lord," across the sky.
I'd like to give bluebonnets to people I've never met
        and blackberries to people I've never liked
        and laughter to everyone.
I'd like to give my love and my life to you, Lord.

acknowledgments

photo credits

Cover—Don Heath; page 1—*Sports Illustrated* photo by Heinz Kluetmeier ©Time, Inc.
 4—Wide World Photo; 6—Art Montgomery; 8-9—Harold M. Lambert;
10—UPI photo; 13—*Los Angeles Times;* 14—Don Heath;
16-17—*Sports Illustrated* photo by John G. Zimmerman ©Time, Inc.
19—Art Montgomery; 20-21—Wide World Photo; 22—*Los Angeles Times;*
24-25—*Sports Illustrated* photo by Leviton-Atlanta, ©Time, Inc.
26-27—*Los Angeles Times;* 29—*Sports Illustrated* photo by T. Tanuma ©Time, Inc.
30—Dennis Osterlund, c/o Aqua-Sport, Goteborg, Sweden; 33—Helen M. Drysdale;
34—Wide World Photo; 37—*Sports Illustrated* photo by Heinz Kluetmeier ©Time, Inc.
39—Harry J. Seaman; 41—Wide World Photo; 42—*Los Angeles Times;*
44-45—Al Zdenek, M.D.; 46-47—Don Heath; 48—*Los Angeles Times;*
51—Herbert Migdoll; 52—Todd Friedman, *Tennis West* magazine; 54-55—UPI;
56—*Sports Illustrated* photo by Neil Leifer ©Time, Inc.;
58—Don Ornitz, Globe Photos, Inc.; 61—Barbara Morgan, Time, Inc.
62—UPI photo; 64-65—Kasti Rushomaa from Black Star;
66—Ringling Bros. and Barnum & Bailey Combined Shows, Inc.
69—*Los Angeles Times;* 70—*Los Angeles Times;* 72—UPI photo; 74—Don Heath;
76-77—Helen M. Drysdale; 78—Ringling Bros. and Barnum & Bailey Combined Shows, Inc.
80—Wide World Photo; 82-83—William Alan Shirley; 85—Robert E. Lapavor;
86—*Los Angeles Times;* 88-89—*Sports illustrated* photo by Eric Schweikardt ©Time, Inc.
90—Don Heath; back cover flap (photos of Marge and Marilee) William Alan Shirley.

layout and design/Ronald Patterson